FOREVER COMMITTED

Building Marriages That Last Through Faith, Truth, and Sacrifice

Alan & Sobreta Harris

Copyright © 2025 Alan & Sobreta Harris

All rights reserved.

No part of this publication may be reproduced, distributed, or transmitted in any form or by any means, including photocopying, recording, or other electronic or mechanical methods, without the prior written permission of the authors, except in the case of brief quotations embodied in critical reviews and certain other noncommercial uses permitted by copyright law.

Alan and Sobreta Harris

forevercommittedmm@gmail.com

Cover Design by Yvette Cage

Author Photo by TreVoy Kelly Photography

ISBN: 979-8-9994461-0-7

DEDICATION

To every couple fighting to keep their vows,
To the ones who choose to stay when leaving seems easier,
To the ones who pray together, cry together, grow together—
This book is for you.
May you be reminded that love is a decision, not just a feeling,
And that commitment is not a cage, but a covenant.
Stay in it.
Stand on it.
Remain Forever Committed.

FOREWORD

By Bishop Shelton Bady

Alan and Sobreta Harris are a passionate and purpose-driven couple. Their intensity comes not just from emotion, but from a deep commitment to fulfilling the assignments God has placed on their lives.

I've had the privilege of witnessing their faithful service in ministry over the years. What stands out most is how their connection with God anchors everything they do. Their love for one another spills over into the way they treat others - with respect, grace, and genuine care.

Through years of experience, the Harrises have gained rich insight and spiritual wisdom. Their journey equips them to guide couples who long for marriages that are not only happy, but purpose filled. Alan leads with strength and humility, never imposing but always inviting. Sobreta's wit and wisdom have a way of disarming resistance and opening hearts to truth. Together, they offer practical tools and spiritual guidance to help build homes that reflect God's design.

My prayer is that everyone who reads this book will experience multiplied grace and favor in their relationships - and be inspired to pursue a forever commitment rooted in faith, truth, and sacrificial love.

Bishop Shelton Bady,
Legacy Pastor - The Harvest Church

A SECOND FOREWORD

By Elders Virginia & William Franklin

Over the past two decades my husband William and I, who have been joyfully married for 39 years, have had the honor of walking alongside Sobreta and Alan "Wayne" Harris. They are two people whose lives reflect the very message they share in this book. We have witnessed their journey of becoming a blended family, raising six children in the nurturing and transformative love of God. Through the years, they have modeled what it means to build a Christ-centered home, grounded not in perfection, but in purpose, prayer, and perseverance.

Forever Committed is not just a book, it's a testimony. The Harris' marriage exemplifies the sacred covenant God intended between husband and wife, echoing the love Christ has for His church. Their words are not theoretical. They are lived, tested, and proven.

As you turn these pages, prepare to be encouraged, challenged, and inspired. Whether you're preparing for marriage, rebuilding one, or seeking to deepen the bond you already cherish, Sobreta and Wayne offer wisdom rooted in Scripture and strengthened by experience. We wholeheartedly support and celebrate this work, knowing it will bless many marriages just as their lives have blessed ours.

"Though one may be overpowered, two can defend themselves. A cord of three strands is not quickly broken."
— Ecclesiastes 4:12 (NIV)

A Prayer:
Heavenly Father, thank You for the example of Sobreta and Wayne Harris. May every couple who read this book be drawn closer to one another and ultimately closer to You. Strengthen marriages, restore hope, and let Your love be the foundation of every home. In Jesus' name, Amen.

Elders Virginia and William Franklin
Marriage Ministry Advisors - The Potters House of Dallas

PREFACE

When we set out to write this book, we didn't just want to share advice, we want to share our hearts. *Forever Committed* was born from real experiences, real conversations, and a real desire to see marriages thrive—not just survive.

Over the years, we have walked through seasons of joy and seasons of pain. We have counseled couples on the brink of giving up and celebrated with others as they renewed their love and commitment. We have made mistakes, learned from them, and watched God use our journey as a testimony for His glory. That's what this book is: a collection of truths and insights God taught us through it all.

This is not a list of perfect answers or a rulebook for marriage. It is a companion for the couple who want more, more unity, more connection, more purpose. It is for those who believe that marriage still matters. That covenant still holds weight. That love, when rooted in Christ, truly can last a lifetime.

We wrote *Forever Committed* for you - the couple that's just starting, the couple that's healing, the one that's growing, and even the one barely holding on. Our prayer is that these pages help you fight for your love, anchor your commitment in God, and never forget why you said, "I do."

With grace, truth, and hearts full of hope,
Alan & Sobreta Harris

INTRODUCTION

The purpose of this book is to provide thoughtful answers to questions commonly asked by couples at various stages of marriage. Whether you are newlyweds, seasoned couples, or somewhere in between, our hope is that the insights shared in these pages will encourage growth in your relationship and spark meaningful conversations - not debates.

We understand that some of our responses may differ from what others might advise. That's okay. We simply ask that you approach this book with an open heart and an open mind. The wisdom we share is based on our personal journey, shaped by both victories and challenges. We fully recognize that what has worked for us may not work exactly the same way for every couple. Still, we speak from a place of honesty, prayer, and experience.

We are incredibly grateful to God for calling and anointing us for marriage ministry. We did not take lightly the decision to write this book. In fact, it was clear to us that God led us to this assignment. With humility and sincerity, we have prayed over every word, inviting the Holy Spirit to guide our thoughts and responses. Our prayer is that the truths and perspectives found here will benefit not only married couples, but also singles, the divorced, widows and widowers, and anyone preparing for a future marriage.

We love marriage, not just the joy it brings, but the growth it requires. We value the hard conversations, the small daily victories, and the transformative power of commitment. We are passionate about helping others navigate the real-life issues they face in relationships, and we count it a privilege to walk alongside you in this journey.

Our ultimate desire is simple yet profound: to see marriages thrive in unity and purpose. May Forever Committed be a tool that strengthens your bond, deepens your love, and inspires you to reflect the enduring love of Christ in your partnership.

With love and purpose,
Alan and Sobreta Harris

Table of Contents

Acknowledgments — xii

The Purpose of Marriage — 13

Importance of Marriage — 16

The Right Kind of Love — 18

The Power of Association — 21

Love and Respect—In Public and in Private — 24

Loving Communication in Difficult Times — 26

Handle With Care — 28

A Word of Wisdom and Encouragement — 30

Questions & Answers for the Journey — 33

Foundations of a Godly Marriage

    What Is the Key to a Good Marriage? — 34

    Is It Important for the Man To Lead? — 37

    How Important Is It for a Wife to Submit? — 40

    What Does it Mean for a Husband to Love His Wife as Christ Loves the Church? — 43

    What Ways Can You Honor Your Spouse? — 45

    How Much of Yourself and Your Time Should You Give to Your Marriage? — 48

Communication & Connection

    How Do You Get Your Spouse to Better Communicate with You? 50

    Is Learning Your Spouse's Love Language Beneficial? 52

    How Can You Show More Love in Your Marriage? 54

    How Can I Be More Understanding? 57

    How Do You Instill Teamwork in Your Marriage? 59

Intimacy & Trust

    Does a Lack of Sexual Intimacy Mean Your Spouse Doesn't Love You? 61

    How Can We Improve Our Intimacy or Take It to the Next Level? 64

    How Do We Overcome Infidelity in a Marriage? 67

Shared Responsibilities

    How Should a Married Couple Handle Household Responsibilities? 70

    How Should We Discipline Our Children When We Were Raised Differently? 73

    How Important is Financial Stability in Marriage? 76

Family & Faith

    How Important Are Parents to Your Relationship? 78

    Should a Married Couple Be Members of the Same Church? 81

    Can People with Different Religious Beliefs Have a Successful Marriage? 84

Closing Prayer 87

Prayers for Your Marriage	89
Notes & Reflections	95
Conclusion	98
About The Authors	99

ACKNOWLEDGMENTS

First and foremost, we give all glory and honor to God, the true author of love, commitment, and covenant. Without His guidance, strength, and grace, this book - and our marriage - would not be possible.

To our children, our extended family and friends who have supported us, prayed for us, and believed in the ministry of marriage that God placed in our hearts - thank you. Your encouragement has been a light along our journey.

To every couple who asked questions, shared their stories, trials, victories, and lessons - you inspired us. Your openness and willingness to grow gave us hope and confirmed the importance of building marriages on the foundation of faith, truth, and sacrifice.

To the couples who are struggling, learning, rebuilding, or simply holding on - we see you, we are praying for you, and we wrote this book with you in mind. May you find wisdom, healing, and encouragement in these pages.

To our spiritual leaders and mentors who have poured into our lives with love, accountability, and biblical truth - thank you for being vessels of God's voice in our lives and our marriage.

Lastly, to our readers: thank you for allowing us into your hearts and homes. We pray this book encourages, challenges, and blesses you in ways that only God can orchestrate. Stay faithful. Stay committed. Stay forever rooted in His love.

With heartfelt gratitude,
Alan & Sobreta Harris

The Purpose of Marriage
By Alan

I am so thankful to God for surrounding me with friends and family who are not ashamed to publicly display their love through marriage. It's a beautiful testimony that God created marriage to be sacred and joyful. Matthew 5:14 (NKJV) says, "You are the light of the world. A city that is set on a hill cannot be hidden." This verse isn't just referring to us individually as believers - it also applies to every area of our lives, including our marriages. Whether we realize it or not, our marriages are constantly on display. People may not see what happens behind closed doors, but God does. And if you have children or family members living with you, they become firsthand witnesses to your marriage dynamic.

When you're out in public, someone is always observing. Your marriage cannot be hidden. That's why it's so important that our marriages serve as positive testimonies to those who desire to be married. When surrendered to God, our relationships can inspire and encourage others by showing what it looks like to live in peace, unity, joy, selflessness, trust, and mutual respect.
Covering each other in prayer and praying together builds spiritual oneness. Observers need to see that although every marriage faces challenges, looking to God is the key to overcoming them. His way is always the best way, and He can provide answers we don't have on our own.

On the other hand, a negative marital testimony - marked by constant conflict, separation, selfishness, mistrust, and disrespect - can discourage others from desiring marriage altogether. Sadly, many people see marriage as a broken institution because they've never seen it done God's way.
Without God, marriage becomes man-made - a mere arrangement or contract, not a covenant. It becomes a coexistence without spiritual covering, often driven by lust or personal gratification rather than sacrificial love. In this mindset, anything goes — including open

marriages, threesomes, and other perversions that have nothing to do with God's original purpose.

Let me be clear: I'm not speaking from a place of judgment. My heart is to warn, encourage, and enlighten. The enemy is clever - he'll package sin as fun, fantasy, or freedom. But anything that departs from God's design leads to destruction. According to the Bible, marriage was created for procreation within a covenant built on monogamy, love, and sacredness.

Let's look at the definition of sacred (via Wikipedia):

"Devoted or dedicated to a deity or to some religious purpose; consecrated. Entitled to veneration or religious respect by association with divinity or divine things; holy. Pertaining to or connected with religion (opposed to secular or profane)."

Marriage is sacred, not secular. It is not meant to gratify the flesh. Romans 7:18a (NKJV) reminds us, "For I know that in me (that is, in my flesh) nothing good dwells." Marriage must be lived and led through the Spirit, not through our carnal desires.

A Personal Reflection

I was sitting in church during praise and worship when the song "I Need You" began to minister to me deeply. A line from the first verse struck me: "I cannot imagine what my life would be without You." Spiritually speaking, I actually can imagine my life without God - and it would be full of sin, selfishness, and spiritual blindness. Without a Savior, I would be completely lost. Headed straight to hell. But thank God for His grace, mercy, and salvation!

Then I began to think from a marital perspective. Without God at the center of my life, I would never have the strength to withstand the temptations the enemy sends my way. There's no way I could remain successfully married without the help of the Holy Spirit. We need His presence daily to keep us aligned, strengthened, and full of love. There would be no marriage without God. He is the Creator of marriage, and there is no stronger foundation than Him. I believe that every marriage must face challenges to build strength and character - but keeping God at the center is the only way to survive both the trials He allows and the attacks the enemy sends.

Gratitude in the Storms

So, if your marriage has survived arguments, financial strain, trust issues - thank God. If you've come through infidelity, jealousy, rejection - thank God. If you've endured any hardship and your marriage is still standing - thank God. That simply means God has been in the center - holding it all together. Otherwise, you wouldn't have made it this far. And if you're reading this and realize that you've left God out of your marriage - it's not too late.

Submit your marriage under the all-powerful hand of God. Invite Him in through prayer. Dedicate your relationship to His purpose. When you do, your marriage will never be the same - because nothing is impossible with God.

"God created man in His own image...male and female He created them. Then God blessed them, and God said to them, 'Be fruitful and multiply; fill the earth'" —Genesis 1:27, 28, (NKJV)

Reflection Questions:

1. In what ways is your marriage a visible testimony to others?
2. Are you covering your spouse in prayer and seeking God together? If not, what's stopping you?
3. Have you invited God to take the center place in your marriage, or have you unintentionally left Him out?
4. When you face trials in your marriage, do you turn to God together or try to handle them alone?

The Importance of Marriage

By Alan

Marriage is one of the most significant commitments two people can make. It provides a stable, loving, and committed relationship where partners can share their lives, support each other, and grow together. It also serves as the foundation for the family, offering emotional security and often financial benefits as well.

At its core, marriage is about two imperfect people choosing to walk through life together in the bonds of holy matrimony. It's about helping each other become better individuals and stronger partners. A healthy marriage encourages personal growth, emotional support, and mutual encouragement - especially through life's inevitable challenges. Because of its sacred nature, marriage is not something to be taken lightly. Choosing to marry someone should come with serious thought, prayer, and a deep respect for the lifelong vow being made. Each partner should be valued, cherished, and - above all - loved. People are not possessions or steppingstones; they are souls created by God, and they deserve to be treated with dignity and respect.

If a person is not serious about marriage, they should not entertain the idea lightly or lead someone on to believe marriage is the ultimate goal. Emotional manipulation and indecision can cause real harm. Men and women alike have feelings - and those feelings matter. Toying with someone's heart is never acceptable. A relationship that's built on trust, communication, and a strong, healthy foundation is one that's prepared to enter marriage. It requires more than just feelings—it takes commitment, compromise, and a shared vision for the future.

Marriage is not just about romantic love; it's about choosing to love each other every day, even when it's hard. It's about mutual respect, shared responsibility, and a God-centered union that reflects the covenant He intended from the beginning.

"And the Lord God said, 'It is not good that man should be alone; I will make him a helper comparable to him.'" —Genesis 2:18 (NKJV)

Reflection Questions:

1. What role does emotional security play in your relationship or view of marriage?
2. In what ways can you help your spouse (or future spouse) become a better individual?
3. Have you taken time to pray about the seriousness of marriage—either before marrying or while married?
4. Are there any habits or attitudes in your relationship that reflect emotional manipulation or indecision? What can be done to change them?
5. What are some ways you and your spouse can strengthen the foundation of your relationship today?

The Right Kind of Love

By Alan

Ask ten people and you'll probably get ten different answers. Our definitions of love are often shaped by experience - some by joy, others by pain. A simplistic answer, one we often hear, is "God is love." But that phrase carries far more depth than we give it credit for. God is love. But He is also a provider, a healer, joy, strength, a savior. He is everything we need Him to be, exactly when we need it. So, if God is love, then love isn't one-dimensional. It doesn't always look the same. Love is diverse. It adapts. It meets us where we are. In that way, love isn't just a feeling. It's a form of service. It's not static. It transforms and takes on the shape of the people it embraces. And that's exactly what makes love within a marriage both beautiful - and sometimes, challenging.

The Way We Were Taught to Love

I grew up in a household with my parents and two brothers. We were close, no doubt about it. But love in our home was demonstrative, not necessarily verbal or affectionate. We didn't say "I love you" every day, but we showed up for each other. We were there when it mattered.

My dad modeled love through hard work. He believed a man shows love by providing for his family. And he was amazing at it. That definition stuck with me. I carried it into my marriage thinking it was enough - that love expressed through provision and responsibility would always translate.

Then came the realization: my wife saw love differently. Her love was openly affectionate - handholding in the mall, spontaneous phone calls just to say, "I miss you," cuddles on the couch. Beautiful gestures. But to me, it was unfamiliar. These weren't expressions I had grown up with. So, at first, they didn't come naturally. I was faced with a choice. Would I love her my way - the only way I knew? Or would I learn to love her, her way? I chose the latter and that made all the difference.

Implied Love vs. Demonstrative Love

Love, I've learned, tends to fall into two categories: implied and demonstrative. Implied love is subtle. It's in the unspoken: "I'm here for you." "I'm working hard for you." "I've got your back."

Demonstrative love is overt. It speaks aloud. It touches, holds, calls, affirms, and showers affection. Neither is better or worse. But problems arise when we assume the way we love is the way everyone feels loved. That assumption is the enemy of intimacy.

In marriage, we don't get to say, "This is just who I am - deal with it." That's not love. That's convenience dressed up as identity. True love listens. It learns. It adjusts.

Learning to Love Differently

Loving someone the way they desire to be loved isn't always easy. In fact, it may feel unnatural - at first. But that discomfort is actually the evidence of love at work. It means you're stretching, growing, and choosing the other person over your own preference. We often master the parts of love that come naturally to us. But it's the unnatural parts that call for commitment. That's where real growth happens - not just as a spouse, but as a person.

"Compromise is the key. We have the natural part to an art, but we must commit to what's unnatural to us." When you stretch into your spouse's language of love, even if it's foreign to you, it becomes a sacrifice. But it's a joyful one. Because the joy of your spouse becomes your joy, too. And over time, what once felt unnatural becomes second nature.

Agape Love in Action

The highest form of love is agape - unconditional love. It's the kind of love God shows us: sacrificial, selfless, relentless. It's not based on merit or mood. It gives, even when the other hasn't earned it. It serves, even when it isn't returned. "While we were yet sinners, Christ died for us." That, friends, is not natural. But it is divine. And it is our model.

Marriage is our opportunity to reflect that kind of love. Not just when it's easy, but especially when it's not. Not just when it comes instinctively, but when it calls for sacrifice, humility, and growth. So, I'll say this clearly:

Love your spouse according to how they feel loved. Not just how you were taught to love. Not just what feels comfortable. But in a way that reflects Christ - who gave, and gave, and gave… for us.

"Above all, clothe yourselves with love, which binds us all together in perfect harmony." —Colossians 3:14 (NKJV)

Reflection Questions:

1. How did your upbringing shape the way you give and receive love?
2. In what ways does your spouse's love language differ from yours?
3. What's one "unnatural" way of loving your spouse that you can commit to practicing this week?
4. How can your marriage reflect the selfless love of Christ more fully?

The Power of Association

By Alan

Whether we realize it or not, there is undeniable power in association.

One of the clearest ways to see this power at work is through the lens of society.

Imagine a kid raised in a loving home with solid values, good parents, and a promising future. Most people would look at that kid and assume success is just around the corner. But let that same kid start spending time with known troublemakers - criminals with no sense of direction - and suddenly, the narrative shifts. Society begins to label that once-promising child as one of them.

Why? Because who you associate with influences not only your behavior but also how others perceive you.

We've all heard a concerned parent say, "I don't want you hanging around that kid." Or maybe, "That group is nothing but trouble." They understand something critical: you are who you surround yourself with.

Association in Marriage

If we're being honest, most of our thinking follows the logic of popular belief and social influence. And if that's true, then we must apply that same principle to our marriages.

If we desire marriages that are strong, fruitful, and built to last, then we must surround ourselves with couples who reflect those very qualities. It doesn't mean those couples are perfect. Far from it. But they are resilient. They face adversity together. They fight fair. They speak the truth in love. And perhaps most importantly, they've taken the option of "leaving" off the table.

These are the kinds of couples who walk in transparency, who operate in truth, and who hold each other - and others - accountable. They don't tell you what you want to hear. They tell you what you need to hear. That kind of association is powerful.

Upward and Outward

We should always keep two kinds of couples in our relational circle:

1. Couples we look up to. They help us continue to grow, challenge us to be better, and model what healthy, Kingdom-minded marriage looks like.
2. Couples we can pour into. Those who may be newer in marriage or facing tough seasons, who need encouragement, wisdom, and truth from someone who's a little further down the road.

This upward and outward dynamic is crucial - not just for our personal growth, but for the strength of the Body of Christ. It gives witness to the power and purpose of marriage. It proclaims that God's design works when we work it, and when we walk in community.

Iron Sharpens Iron

The Bible says, "Iron sharpens iron, so one person sharpens another." (Proverbs 27:17 NIV)

When we associate with strong, Christ-centered couples, we sharpen one another. We're encouraged, corrected, inspired, and supported. We become better, not just by instruction, but by example.

Instead of feeling intimidated by couples who seem to have it together, we should lean in. Learn from them. Fellowship with them. Invite accountability. Let their testimony stretch your Perspective: and raise your standard. The truth is: if you hang around successful couples, you will begin to reflect on their success.

You'll begin to see what's possible. You'll believe for more for your own marriage. You'll adopt habits and attitudes that lead to fruitfulness. And eventually, others will look at your marriage and see the difference too.

That's the Power of Association - and when it's rooted in Christ, it can radically transform your marriage from the inside out.

Behold, how good and pleasant it is when brothers dwell in unity! — Psalm 133:1 (ESV)

With all humility and gentleness, with patience, bearing with one another in love, eager to maintain the unity of the Spirit in the bond of peace. —Ephesians 4:2-3 (ESV)

Reflection Questions:

1. What couples are currently in your inner circle? Do they reflect the kind of marriage you desire?
2. Are you allowing others to speak truth into your relationship - even when it's uncomfortable?
3. Is there a couple you can begin mentoring or walking alongside?
4. What intentional steps can you take this month to fellowship with stronger couples?

Love and Respect—In Public and in Private

By Sobreta

Spouses, be sure to treat each other with love and respect in public and behind closed doors! Your spouse should feel safe, cherished, and valued - whether there's an audience or it's just the two of you. One of the most damaging things you can do in a marriage is dishonor your spouse in front of others or make them feel unseen or unwanted in private.

Please do not shut your spouse out when you're going through hard times. Those are the moments when you need each other the most. Isolation during trials only creates greater emotional distance and confusion. Marriage was designed by God as a partnership. That means both spouses lean on each other, pray for each other, and walk through every season - good and bad - together.

Your spouse is more than just a roommate or co-parent. They are your best friend, your listening ear, your confidant, your prayer partner, and when appropriate, your advisor. Don't suffer in silence. Share your heart and your concerns. Because whatever affects you will ultimately affect your spouse, and if it's not addressed, it can strain the entire marriage.

Communication is key. And not just any kind of communication - effective communication. Yelling, hollering, and screaming never lead to understanding; they create fear, defensiveness, and distance. Speak the truth in love. Be quick to listen, slow to speak, and slow to anger. When both spouses feel heard and respected, intimacy and trust deepen.

Let's also be reminded of God's design for marriage:

"Wives, submit to your own husbands, as is fitting in the Lord. Husbands, love your wives and do not be bitter toward them." — Colossians 3:18–19 (NKJV)

Reflection Questions:

1. In what ways do you honor or dishonor your spouse in public and in private? What changes might God be prompting you to make?
2. Does your spouse feel emotionally safe with you? What specific actions or words can help build a stronger sense of security in your relationship?
3. How well are you currently communicating with your spouse? Are you more focused on being heard or on truly listening?
4. How do you usually handle conflict in your marriage? Do you raise your voice, shut down, or pursue peace through prayer and conversation?

Loving Communication in Difficult Times

By Sobreta

When your spouse is going through something, that is not the time to turn your back on them. That is the time to turn toward each other, to press in with love, support, and prayer. A spouse is not your enemy - they are your partner. You live with them, not against them.

In moments of frustration, we must be careful not to take our emotions out on our spouse. Instead, turn to your spouse in prayer. Ask them to walk with you spiritually, emotionally, and practically. Frustrating one another only breeds division and robs the relationship of peace. Deal with the issue together, not by fighting about it. Seek God daily for a greater level of love and understanding in your marriage.

Stop holding things in. Learn how to talk about what's bothering you - not with blame, yelling, or disrespect - but with patience, gentleness, and love. We are called to consistently operate in love toward our spouses. Communication is not about control; it's about connection.

True communication involves two people: one speaking, and the other listening. Both should feel heard. Both should feel safe. Both should feel respected. It's also okay to ask questions to gain clarity - but don't demand answers in a way that dishonors your spouse's heart.

Saying things like, "Just say yes or no," or "Cut out the details," may feel efficient in the moment, but they're often deeply hurtful. When we try to control how our spouse responds, we stifle intimacy and silence the very heart we vowed to protect.

God is not pleased with that kind of interaction. It does not reflect His nature or His command to love one another unconditionally. Let's communicate in ways that mirror His love - kind, patient, and full of grace.

"A gentle answer turns away wrath, but a harsh word stirs up anger."
—Proverbs 15:1 (NIV)

"Be completely humble and gentle; be patient, bearing with one another in love." —Ephesians 4:2 (NIV)

Reflection Questions:

1. When your spouse is going through a difficult time, do you press in with love and support - or tend to pull away? How can you show up better this week?
2. In moments of frustration or stress, are you inviting your spouse to walk with you - or unintentionally pushing them away? What might it look like to turn to them in prayer instead?
3. Think back to a recent disagreement: did you listen to understand or just to respond? What can you do differently to foster safer, more respectful communication?

Handle With Care

By Sobreta

A marriage should be meaningful - not merely a shared last name between two people living under the same roof. A married couple should nurture their relationship and continue to grow in love, not simply settle for mediocrity. Love should be expressed often, both in words and in actions. Being married is not the goal - cultivating a loving, God-honoring relationship is.

When the honeymoon phase fades, life gets hard, and the pressures of daily living set in, couples must resist the temptation to withdraw. This is the time to draw closer, to stand together, and to lean on God. The joy you once shared should not vanish because of difficulties or the passage of time.

No marriage is meant to simply exist. A thriving marriage is marked by love, honest communication, mutual understanding, unity, joy, laughter, physical closeness, trust, shared responsibility, and healthy conflict resolution. When these qualities are missing, one or both spouses may begin to feel unloved, unwanted, and unappreciated.

We must be intentional about keeping the fire burning. Marriage is a God-ordained covenant, and because of its significance, the enemy works hard to bring division. Often, he doesn't need to do much - just stir up circumstances. In those moments, we must be careful not to let those circumstances use us to destroy what God has built.

Let your spouse know how much you love, need, and cherish them. Remind them that you're grateful to share life with them. Showing up daily - emotionally, spiritually, and practically - lets them know that your marriage is a priority.

Ask yourself: What am I actively doing to keep our marriage strong? How am I ensuring my spouse feels safe, secure, and wanted? Do my words clearly communicate how much I care?

Marriage is honorable before God. Your spouse is not just your partner - they are a gift from the Lord. And like any valuable gift, they must be handled with care. Many tangible gifts come with care instructions. Have you taken time to learn your spouse's?

A healthy, thriving marriage is built on two people who intentionally choose - day after day - to handle one another with love, care, and deep respect.

"Wives, in the same way submit yourselves to your own husbands so that, if any of them do not believe the word, they may be won over without words by the behavior of their wives, when they see the purity and reverence of your lives." —1st Peter 3:1, 2 (NIV)

"Husbands, in the same way be considerate as you live with your wives, and treat them with respect as the weaker partner and as heirs with you of the gracious gift of life, so that nothing will hinder your prayers. Finally, all of you be of one mind, having compassion for one another; love as brothers, be tenderhearted, be [a]courteous;" —1st Peter 3:7, 8 (NIV)

Reflection Questions:

1. Have I allowed life's pressures to distance me from my spouse, or have I used those moments to draw closer and grow stronger together?
2. Do I regularly express appreciation and affection, or have I grown complacent in our connection?
3. Have I taken the time to truly learn my spouse's emotional and physical "care instructions"? How well am I honoring them?
4. How can I better reflect God's heart in the way I speak to, serve, and cherish my spouse daily?

A Word of Wisdom and Encouragement

By Sobreta

Marriage is a sacred union created by God. The Bible emphasizes just how important it is. When someone enters into marriage without understanding its significance - or without honoring God's Word - unnecessary pain and brokenness can result. That's why it's so important to approach marriage with reverence, humility, and maturity.

To the women who are waiting on God for a husband: I lovingly encourage you to wait patiently and trust God's perfect timing. While you're waiting, seek Him wholeheartedly. Stay pure in heart, mind, and body. Focus on the purpose He has for you in this season. God's plan is always better than anything we could orchestrate ourselves.

Believe me, you want to be with the man that God has chosen and prepared for you—someone who honors God and is ready to love you well. Trust that God won't lead you to someone else's husband or to a man who is already entangled in another relationship, whether troubled or not. God is not the author of confusion. He will not bless a relationship built on deception, secrecy, or disobedience to His Word.

If you find yourself in a situation where emotions are involved with someone who isn't yours, I say this in love: pause and surrender it to God. Pray for clarity. Ask God to guard your heart and not allow you to develop feelings for someone who isn't meant to be your husband. And remember, when Scripture says, *"He who finds a wife..."* it doesn't mean you have to chase or entice anyone. Be the woman God has called you to be and let Him do the connecting in His perfect way and time.

For the men, especially husbands, I say this with great care: there's a real enemy who wants to destroy you, your purpose, and your marriage. If you're not walking in God's will, it's easy to unknowingly open the door to attacks that can bring damage to your home. As husbands, God has entrusted you with the responsibility to lead, protect, and cover your wife in love and prayer. When distractions arise - whether from within or outside of your marriage - lean into God, not temptation. Be mindful of relationships that don't honor your covenant. Any connection that jeopardizes your marriage is not from God.

I share all of this not to condemn, but to help. Marriage isn't easy, it's a daily commitment to love, serve, forgive, and grow. But it's also a beautiful blessing when built on God's foundation. If you're struggling, don't act out of frustration or fear. Pray. Seek God's guidance. Invite Him into your situation before you take matters into your own hands.

To all - married or single - don't let the distractions of the enemy pull you away from God's best for your life. This message has been on my heart, and I truly hope it encourages the person reading this. My prayer is for marriages to thrive, for hearts to heal, and for lives to be aligned with God's will.

If this doesn't apply to you personally but it brings someone else to mind, please consider sharing it. You never know how your obedience might be the lifeline someone needs.

Let's choose to honor God in our relationships. Let's choose love, truth, and integrity.

"Therefore what God has joined together, let not man separate." — Mark 10:9 (NKJV)

"Marriage is honorable among all, and the bed undefiled; but fornicators and adulterers God will judge." —Hebrews 13:4 (NKJV)

Reflection Questions:

1. Am I honoring the sacredness of marriage—whether I'm currently married or waiting for marriage? What does that look like in my daily decisions, thoughts, and actions?
2. Have I invited God into every area of my relationship (or desire for a relationship)? What areas might I still be holding back?
3. Am I seeking God's will above my own desires when it comes to love and relationships? Have I been honest with God about my struggles or feelings?
4. Is there any relationship in my life that I need to reevaluate in light of God's Word? Am I willing to surrender anything that is not pleasing to God?
5. As a spouse, am I walking in alignment with God's design for my role in the marriage?

Questions & Answers

Real Conversations. Real Commitment.

"Plans fail for lack of counsel, but with many advisers they succeed."
—Proverbs 15:22 (NIV)

In this section, we answer real questions from real people—based on our experiences, biblical truths, and the lessons we've learned along the way. Our hope is that our transparency encourages you, challenges you, and helps your marriage thrive.

What Is the Key to a Good Marriage?

Sobreta's Perspective:

I believe the key to a good marriage is the commitment and willingness to fulfill your spousal role with love and understanding. Each spouse should desire to make the relationship work by being thoughtful, intentional, and loving. A good marriage thrives when both individuals are committed to making it meaningful and lasting.

Marriage isn't always easy, and it's certainly not perfect. Each spouse must enter it knowing that challenges will come and that neither person is flawless. There will be times without laughter, and moments of discomfort that require patience and prayer to resolve. Every marriage faces its own unique struggles, no two are alike. Still, marriage remains a beautiful gift from God. "With all lowliness and gentleness, with longsuffering, bearing with one another in love, endeavoring to keep the unity of the Spirit in the bond of peace."—Ephesians 4:2–3 (NKJV)

The commitment to walk together through whatever life brings—while leaning on the Holy Spirit for guidance—strengthens the union over time. Praying for one another, with one another, and asking God to help you be the best spouse you can be is essential for a marriage to grow and thrive. "Two are better than one, because they have a good reward for their labor. For if they fall, one will lift up his companion."—Ecclesiastes 4:9–10 (NKJV)

Alan's Perspective:

The key to a good marriage is proper communication. It's the only way to clearly express your needs, set expectations, and nurture a healthy relationship. Communication ensures that your needs aren't left unmet and that both spouses feel heard, understood, and valued. "Let every man be swift to hear, slow to speak, slow to wrath."—James 1:19 (NKJV)

Through effective communication, you teach your spouse what brings you joy and what causes discomfort. It also helps establish healthy boundaries, giving clarity about what to initiate and what to avoid. Without open and respectful communication, misunderstandings grow—and intimacy fades. Strong communication builds trust and creates space for true unity. "Let no corrupt word proceed out of your mouth, but what is good for necessary edification, that it may impart grace to the hearers."—Ephesians 4:29 (NKJV)

Our Perspective:

- **Communication is vital.** It's essential for both spouses to listen actively and seek understanding. One speaks while the other listens—without interruption or judgment. Respectful dialogue keeps the connection strong and provides clarity and comfort in every season. "A soft answer turns away wrath, but a harsh word stirs up anger."—Proverbs 15:1 (NKJV)
- **Commitment matters.** A strong marriage is built on two people who are fully committed to one another. This means being faithful to your vows, loving each other through both highs and lows, and choosing to invest in your relationship daily. "Therefore what God has joined together, let not man separate."—Mark 10:9 (NKJV)
- **Meet each other's needs intentionally.** A good marriage requires selflessness. Each spouse should be dedicated to caring for and meeting the other's emotional, physical, and spiritual needs in ways that honor God. "Let each of you look out not only for his own interests, but also for the interests of others."—Philippians 2:4 (NKJV)
- **Keep God first.** A Christ-centered marriage is a strong marriage. Pray together. Study God's Word together. Seek His will in every decision. When God is the foundation, everything else has a better chance of standing firm. "Unless the Lord builds the house, they labor in vain who build it."—Psalm 127:1 (NKJV)

"Nevertheless let each one of you in particular so love his own wife as himself, and let the wife see that she respects her husband." —
Ephesians 5:33 (NKJV)

Reflection Questions:

1. In what ways am I actively showing commitment to my marriage, especially during difficult or less joyful seasons?
2. How well do I communicate my needs, concerns, and appreciation to my spouse? Am I also listening with patience and understanding?
3. Am I intentionally meeting my spouse's emotional, physical, and spiritual needs, or have I become more focused on my own?
4. Is God truly the foundation of our marriage? What can we do to seek Him more consistently—together?

Is It Important for The Man to Lead?

Sobreta's Perspective:

The headship of the husband is of the utmost importance. The husband should lead as he seeks God's will and His way through prayer. His role is to lead his household in a godly manner - not as a ruler or dictator, but as a man after God's own heart.

The husband should lead in such a way that the wife can confidently follow and trust his leadership as he follows God. The Bible declares that the husband is the head of the wife, just as Christ is head of the church. Therefore, he should live a life that honors Christ and pleases the Lord.

Christ loves the church and gave His life for it - and still does. In the same way, the husband should love his wife sacrificially, caring for her, covering her, and protecting her as Christ does.

Alan's Perspective:

There is a divine order to Christian marriage, laid out in **1 Corinthians 11:2–3**: **God the Father → Jesus Christ → Man → Woman.**

Some women may feel unsure about the word *submit* - but let's be clear: submission is not one-sided. Husbands are also called to submit - to **God**. And a man who is truly submitted to God becomes easier to follow.

One of the husband's main responsibilities is to love his wife **unconditionally**, as Christ loves the Church. That means she should always be cherished and have a voice in every decision that impacts the family.

A husband submitted to God will not belittle, harm, or mistreat his wife. Those actions reflect disobedience, not leadership. If both spouses desire a marriage ordained by God, it's worth the sacrifice to obey His Word and enjoy the blessings of His guidance and provision.

Our Perspective:

- God designed marriage with a **divine structure**, and the husband's leadership plays a vital role in that order.
- Leadership in marriage is **not about control**, but about covering, caring, and serving - like Christ leads the Church.
- A godly husband leads from a place of **submission to Christ**, which makes it easier for his wife to trust and follow.
- True leadership means valuing the wife's insight, involving her in decisions, and honoring her voice.
- A husband's love and leadership should be **sacrificial, protective, and consistent**.
- When both spouses walk in their God-given roles, their marriage is positioned to **thrive in unity, peace, and purpose**.

Likewise, husbands, live with your wives in an understanding way, showing honor to the woman as the weaker vessel, since they are heirs with you of the grace of life, so that your prayers may not be hindered. —1 Peter 3:7 ESV

3 But I want you to understand that the head of every man is Christ, the head of a wife is her husband, and the head of Christ is God. —1 Corinthians 11:3 ESV

Reflection Questions:

1. As a husband, am I leading my home in a way that reflects Christ - through humility, sacrifice, and obedience to God?
2. As a wife, do I feel safe and confident trusting my husband's leadership? If not, what needs to be addressed through prayer and communication?
3. How does my current understanding of biblical headship align with God's Word? Have I allowed culture, fear, or past experiences to distort it?

4. In what ways can we grow together as a couple by embracing our God-given roles with love, mutual respect, and spiritual maturity?

How Important Is It for a Wife to Submit?

Sobreta's Perspective:

It is very important for a wife to submit, as stated in **Ephesians 5:22** and **Colossians 3:18**: *"Wives, submit to your own husbands."* The Bible teaches that wives are to submit **as unto the Lord**, meaning she follows her husband's leadership with the same respect and willingness she would offer to God.

Submission is not a curse word, nor should it be viewed as something negative or oppressive. It simply means **following the leadership of a godly husband** who is submitted to the Lord. Submission should be rooted in trust, love, and mutual respect.

Importantly, the wife is not a doormat and is not inferior in any way. She is a **vital and honored partner** in the marriage covenant. When a husband loves his wife as Christ loves the Church, submission becomes much easier and more natural. The Bible also reminds us in **Ephesians 5:21** to submit to one another out of reverence for Christ.

Mutual submission, grounded in love, strengthens the marriage bond.

Alan's Perspective:

It is very important for a wife to submit - **not as a loss of power**, but as an act of faith and obedience to God's divine structure for marriage. Submission positions your marriage for success because it aligns your relationship with God's original blueprint.

God's divine order, as revealed in Scripture, creates balance, unity, and peace. When that order is ignored or flipped, things fall out of alignment - *and what's out of order will eventually break down.*

Submission doesn't mean silence or subservience—it means **trusting the process** God has established and walking in your role with grace, wisdom, and strength. A godly wife submitting to a godly husband reflects the powerful partnership God intended from the beginning.

Our Perspective:

- Submission is **not about control**, but about **alignment with God's divine order**.
- A wife's submission is made easier when her husband **leads in love, humility, and obedience to Christ**.
- The Bible calls both husband and wife to **submit to one another** out of reverence for God.
- **Submission is not weakness** - it's strength under control and a sign of spiritual maturity.
- A wife is **equal in value** but different in function; she is a vital and cherished partner in the marriage.
- When both spouses operate in their biblical roles, the marriage is **blessed with unity, peace, and divine favor**.

"Submit to one another out of reverence for Christ. Wives, submit yourselves to your own husbands as you do to the Lord. For the husband is the head of the wife as Christ is the head of the church, his body, of which he is the Savior. Now as the church submits to Christ, so also wives should submit to their husbands in everything. In this same way, husbands ought to love their wives as their own bodies. He who loves his wife loves himself. After all, no one ever hated their own body, but they feed and care for their body, just as Christ does the church, for we are members of his body." —Ephesians 5:21-24; 28-30

Reflection Questions:

1. Do I view submission as a spiritual act of trust in God's order, or have past experiences shaped a negative view of it?
2. Am I (as a wife) walking in submission with grace and strength, or do I find myself resisting my husband's leadership—even when it aligns with God's Word?

3. How does mutual submission play out in our marriage? Are we both honoring one another in love and humility?
4. In what ways can I help cultivate a marriage where biblical roles are respected, and both spouses feel valued and secure?

What Does It Mean for A Husband to Love His Wife as Christ Loves the Church?

Alan's Perspective:

To love your wife as Christ loves the Church means to lead her with compassion, cover her in prayer, and be willing to sacrifice for her without hesitation. Christ gave His life for the Church, that's the model. Leadership in marriage is not about being a dictator; it's about being a servant-leader. A husband's love should be evident in his words, actions, decisions, and the way he nurtures his wife emotionally and spiritually.

This type of love creates an environment where submission is not demanded - it's given freely because it's safe. Loving leadership listens, protects, corrects gently, and prioritizes the well-being of the wife above personal convenience. When I love my wife this way, I'm not just being a good husband, I'm honoring God.

Sobreta's Perspective:

When a husband truly loves his wife as Christ loves the Church, it brings peace and security to the marriage. It becomes easier for the wife to follow her husband's lead when she knows his heart is for her and his decisions are being guided by God. This type of love is sacrificial - it doesn't seek its own benefit but considers what's best for the whole family.

Christ's love is patient, forgiving, and never abusive or harsh. So, when a husband walks in that kind of love, it reflects the heart of God in the home. That's the kind of love that makes a wife feel seen, valued, and covered. It builds intimacy and trust.

Our Perspective:

- **Loving leadership** is rooted in sacrifice, not superiority.

- **When a husband leads with love**, it invites unity, peace, and trust into the marriage.
- The husband's role is not to control, but to cover and **care for his wife** spiritually, emotionally, and physically.
- **Christ is the model.** He laid down His life for the Church - husbands are called to carry that same level of devotion for their wives.
- Leadership without love creates resistance; leadership with love invites submission.
- When both spouses walk in their God-given roles, marriage becomes a powerful reflection of God's covenant love.

"Husbands, love your wives, just as Christ also loved the church and gave Himself for her, that He might [g]sanctify and cleanse her with the washing of water by the word, that He might present her to Himself a glorious church, not having spot or wrinkle or any such thing, but that she should be holy and without blemish. So husbands ought to love their own wives as their own bodies; he who loves his wife loves himself." —Ephesians 5: 25 – 28 NKJV

Reflection Questions:

1. Am I leading my wife with Christlike love - marked by compassion, sacrifice, and spiritual covering - or am I leading from pride or control?
2. How do my words, actions, and decisions make my wife feel emotionally and spiritually? Does she feel safe, seen, and supported?
3. In what ways am I reflecting Christ's heart in my marriage—especially during moments of conflict, stress, or disagreement?
4. How can I grow as a servant-leader in my home, and what steps can I take to better love my wife as Christ loves the Church?

What Ways Can You Honor Your Spouse?

Sobreta's Perspective:

As a wife, you can honor your husband by submitting to him as Scripture instructs in *Ephesians 5:22* and *Colossians 3:18*, while he submits to the Lord. Submission, when done biblically, is not oppression—it is a posture of respect, support, and partnership. Honor your husband by praying for him daily, by serving him in ways that align with his desires, and by affirming him with your words and actions.

Husbands honor their wives by loving them as Christ loves the Church, which is a sacrificial, nurturing, and unconditional kind of love (*Ephesians 5:25, Colossians 3:19*). Honor also comes through encouragement, motivation, and uplifting one another with genuine compliments and positivity.

Another important way to honor each other is by valuing your spouse's thoughts and feelings during decision-making. Honor is shown when you include your spouse in your personal decisions, making them feel seen, respected, and valued.

Speak highly of your spouse when they are not present and speak to them with love and kindness when others are watching. Public and private respect both carry weight. Favor your spouse above all others and let your actions reflect that commitment. Honor is in the details, in how you prioritize, support, and cherish your spouse every day.

Alan's Perspective:

There are many meaningful ways to honor your spouse, and at the foundation of all of them is **your relationship with God**. Placing God at the center of your marriage gives you the grace and strength to honor your spouse in ways that go beyond human ability. That includes **unconditional love, forgiveness, patience, and humility**, all of which are extremely difficult to maintain without divine help.

Some essential traits that demonstrate honor in marriage include:

- **Accountability** – Being transparent and responsible for your actions.
- **Commitment** – Staying true to your vows and remaining present through every season.
- **Emotional Support** – Being your spouse's biggest fan and a safe place to land.
- **Trustworthiness** – Creating an environment of security and integrity.
- **Prioritizing Your Spouse** – Choosing your spouse above friends, hobbies, or even extended family.

Another meaningful way to honor your spouse is by **celebrating them intentionally** - remember birthdays, anniversaries, milestones, and achievements. These celebrations send a strong message: *"You matter to me. You are worth honoring."*

Our Perspective:

- **Being accountable to your spouse** shows them they are valued and respected.
- **Putting your spouse first** is a daily act of honor.
- **Committing fully** to your marriage and making choices that protect and nurture your union displays deep honor.
- **Applying biblical principles** such as love, patience, humility, and grace strengthens your relationship and shows reverence for God and for one another.
- **Demonstrating unconditional love** is a powerful expression of honor, especially during challenging times.

"Let marriage be held in honor among all, and let the marriage bed be undefiled, for God will judge the sexually immoral and adulterous." —Hebrews 13:4 (ESV)

Reflection Questions:

1. In what specific ways have I recently honored my spouse with my words and actions? How did it impact them? Do I speak about my spouse with honor and respect when they are not around? If not, why?
2. Am I accountable in my marriage? In what ways can I be more transparent, consistent, or dependable?
3. How often do I include my spouse in decision-making? Do they feel heard and valued when I make important choices?
4. Do I celebrate my spouse's accomplishments and milestones with intentionality? How can I improve in this area?

How Much of Yourself and Your Time Should You Give to Your Marriage?

Sobreta's Perspective:

Each spouse should give **one hundred percent** of themselves to the marriage. This means wholeheartedly embracing the ideals, purpose, and meaning of marriage. It does **not** mean losing yourself or your identity—but it **does** mean that two whole people are choosing to become one. Combining your ideals, dreams, and goals into one union is a beautiful thing. *"So then, they are no longer two but one flesh. Therefore what God has joined together, let not man separate."* —Matthew 19:6 (NKJV)

When you enter marriage with this truth and mindset, you better understand your role - especially as it relates to time. Marriage isn't bondage; it's a chosen union where two people desire to spend their lives together. Therefore, **time together should be cherished.**

If you truly love the one you marry, then you should **desire and enjoy** spending quality time with them. Time spent apart should be for necessary obligations - such as work, school, ministry, or pre-agreed engagements - not because you're trying to live a separate life.

If you're still clinging to a single lifestyle, then you're not ready for marriage. Once married, you are now a **husband or wife**, and you are **accountable to your spouse.**

Alan's Perspective:

In marriage, **it's imperative that both parties give 100% of themselves.** I'm not talking about a 50/50 split—that would mean you're both holding back half of who you are. While it may take time to grow into giving your all - especially early in the marriage - it should **always be the goal.**

Of course, it's not realistic to spend all of your **time** with your spouse due to work, responsibilities, and other obligations. But that's where **balance** comes in. Don't overcommit to outside engagements or activities that consistently rob your marriage of quality time. **Your marriage is a priority**, so treat it as such.

Our Perspective:

- **Give your all** to your marriage—100 percent effort and heart, not just half. Hold nothing back from your spouse.
- **Spend as much quality time** with each other as possible. Quality time is productive, it helps to heal your marriage, and it helps your marriage grow.
- **Balance your time** wisely. You're not just a person with a career - you're a **married** person with a career. Let your marital status shape how you move and make decisions even when your spouse isn't present.
- It's okay to **have personal time**, too. Personal time is important for self-growth, reflection, and restoration - as long as it doesn't pull you away from your marital responsibilities.

"Be devoted to one another in love. Honor one another above yourselves." – Romans 12:10 (NIV)

Reflection Questions:

1. Am I giving my whole self - emotionally, mentally, spiritually - to my marriage, or am I holding something back?
2. What does "quality time" look like for us as a couple? Are we spending enough of it together?
3. Are there any outside commitments that consistently take time and energy away from our marriage? If so, how can I adjust or reprioritize?
4. Do I view time with my spouse as a joy or a duty? How can I cultivate more joy and intentionality in our time together?
5. How can we better balance personal time and couple time without neglecting either?

How Do You Get Your Spouse to Better Communicate with You?

Sobreta's Perspective:

Communication is one of the foundations for a strong and lasting marriage. Both spouses should be **willing to learn** how to be effective communicators. Communication was never intended to be one-sided—**it requires effort from both people.**

One of the most important keys to good communication is being a **good listener**. Another key is making sure you **understand what your spouse is communicating**. Without understanding, true communication cannot happen. Both partners must commit to **respecting each other's opinions and concerns** and be intentional about listening.

"Wisdom is the principal thing; therefore get wisdom. And in all your getting, get understanding." —Proverbs 4:7 (NKJV)

Alan's Perspective:

Proper communication doesn't come naturally to everyone. We all have different upbringings and communication styles—some effective, others not so much. If there's a breakdown in communication, **don't try to force it** or demand change overnight.

There are many ways to grow in this area. **Marriage books, seminars, and counseling** can provide tools and insights that lead to more effective conversations. Be patient and lead by example. **Frustration only fuels tension** and can lead to unnecessary conflict. Keep in mind that everyone **learns and processes differently**, so be gracious while your spouse learns how to communicate better.

Our Perspective:

- **Be clear and respectful** when communicating. If emotions are high, hit pause until both of you can talk calmly and respectfully.
- **Take your time** during discussions. The goal is for both spouses to fully understand what is being said.
- **Be an active listener.** A good listener pays attention, seeks to understand, and responds with love and care.
- **Pray first.** Invite the Holy Spirit into your conversation. He will guide your words and help bring clarity and peace.
- **Seek professional support** if communication becomes overwhelming or consistently leads to conflict.
- **Invest in your growth.** Books, conferences, and seminars are great tools to sharpen your communication skills as a couple.

"Let no corrupting talk come out of your mouths, but only such as is good for building up, as fits the occasion, that it may give grace to those who hear." —Ephesians 4:29 (ESV)

Reflection Questions:

1. Am I creating a safe and respectful environment where my spouse feels comfortable opening up to me?
2. How well do I listen when my spouse is speaking? Do I listen to understand—or to respond?
3. Have I taken steps to improve my own communication habits before expecting change from my spouse?
4. Are we inviting God into our conversations through prayer and seeking wisdom when communication feels difficult?

Is Learning Your Spouse's Love Language Beneficial to your Marriage?

Sobreta's Perspective:

Learning your spouse's love language is absolutely beneficial to your marriage because it strengthens and enhances your relationship. It creates space for more **intimacy, joy, and peace** in your union. When you intentionally meet your spouse's needs in ways that speak directly to their heart, it demonstrates how important they are to you.

Knowing each other's love language promotes deeper **understanding and connection**. It teaches both partners how to **love intentionally**, and how to avoid habits or actions that might be unhelpful or even hurtful. When a spouse's love language is neglected or ignored, it can lead to distance, discontent, or disconnection in the relationship.

Every couple should take time to complete the **Love Language test**, not just to learn their own, but to also discover how their spouse experiences love. **That knowledge is only helpful when it is shared and practiced.** Keeping it to yourself defeats the purpose.

Alan's Perspective:

Learning your spouse's love language is a game changer in your marriage. It's like discovering a key that opens the door to deeper happiness. Whether it's **Words of Affirmation, Quality Time, Acts of Service, Receiving Gifts, or Physical Touch**, these five love languages are powerful tools designed to help you meet your spouse's needs in a meaningful way.

There are simple, free assessments online that will help you identify your love language and your spouse's. When you both know which language speaks love to the other, you can communicate more effectively and **create a loving atmosphere that feels fulfilling and safe**. It's not just about knowing it—it's about **putting it into**

practice. Learning and using your spouse's love language shows you care enough to love them the way they want and need to be loved.

Our Perspective:

- **Take the Love Language assessment** together and talk about the results.
- **Put what you learn into practice daily.** Don't wait for a special occasion.
- **Be creative** in how you express your spouse's love language. Add your own personal touch.
- **Take it seriously.** Understanding love languages is a powerful way to deepen connection and unity in your marriage.

"Love is patient and kind; love does not envy or boast; it is not arrogant or rude. It does not insist on its own way; it is not irritable or resentful; it does not rejoice at wrongdoing but rejoices with the truth. Love bears all things, believes all things, hopes all things, endures all things." —1 Corinthians 13:4–7 (ESV)

Reflection Questions:

1. Have I taken time to learn and understand my spouse's love language and am I consistently speaking it?
2. How does my spouse typically respond when I show love in ways that are meaningful to them?
3. Are there habits I need to change because they conflict with my spouse's love language or make them feel unseen?
4. What practical steps can I take this week to express love more intentionally, based on what my spouse truly needs?

How Can You Show More Love in Your Marriage?

Sobreta's Perspective:

True love originates from God. The Bible says that *"God is love"* (1 John 4:8), and when we allow His love to flow through us, it becomes easier to love our spouse unconditionally. Each spouse should be intentional about displaying love in their heart **daily and sincerely**.

I recall something Bishop Shelton Bady once suggested at Harvest Time Church that has stayed with me for years: he encouraged married couples to **add to their morning prayer a request for God to show them how to please their spouse that day**. This simple yet powerful prayer opens the heart to divine guidance and leads to meaningful acts of love, tailored uniquely for your spouse.

At times, a spouse may believe they are loved but still **feel unseen or emotionally disconnected**. This is where honest and compassionate communication becomes essential. If one spouse is expressing love but the other doesn't feel it, something may be missing in the expression or reception of that love.

Ask thoughtful questions like:

- *How can I be a better wife/husband?*
- *What makes you feel most loved by me?*

You can also show more love by **supporting your spouse's dreams, talents, and goals**, and by being consistently present through the good and the bad. Take time to discuss what love looks like to each of you, as it often means different things to different people. Then, ask God to lead you in showing love according to what your spouse needs - not just what you're used to giving.

Alan's Perspective:

To show more love in your marriage, you need to **prioritize your**

marriage, make it one of the most important parts of your life. A loving marriage doesn't happen by accident; it takes **consistent, intentional effort.**

Start by **being present and emotionally available.** When your spouse sees that you are invested in their emotional and spiritual well-being, it shows that you truly care. Love is demonstrated not just through words, but through action.

You can also **invest in your marriage by seeking out resources** that strengthen your bond. Read marriage books, attend seminars, participate in retreats, and surround yourselves with couples who are building strong, godly marriages.

Finally, never underestimate the power of **fun and connection.** Enjoy regular date nights, take trips together, and create new experiences. These shared moments reignite joy and strengthen your bond.

Our Perspective:

- **Be intentional** about giving emotional support - it's one of the clearest ways to show love.
- **Make your spouse a priority.** Love thrives where there is focused attention.
- **Start your day with prayer**, asking God to reveal how you can love your spouse better today.
- **Show up** - emotionally, physically, and spiritually. Being present matters.

"Let all that you do be done in love." —1 Corinthians 16:14 (ESV)

Reflection Questions:

1. How do I most naturally show love to my spouse?
   (Is it through words, service, gifts, touch, or quality time?)

2. What specific actions or words make me feel most loved by my spouse?
   (Be as detailed as possible—little things matter.)
3. In what ways could I be more intentional about showing love to my spouse each day?
4. Are there times when I feel unloved, even though I know my spouse loves me? Why might that be?
5. What can I ask God to help me with in becoming a more loving husband/wife?

How Can I Be More Understanding?

Sobreta's Perspective:

The Bible says, *"In all thy getting, get an understanding."* Understanding your spouse is essential to a healthy marriage, and just as important is communicating effectively so that your spouse can understand you.

Pray and ask God to teach you how to understand your spouse - how to understand their ways, their moods, and their actions. Seek God for wisdom to help you grow in understanding. Wisdom is vital in daily life, and when applied to marriage, it cultivates love, patience, and concern for your spouse's well-being.

God will respond to a sincere heart. When we seek Him, we learn how to interact with our spouse during emotional or challenging situations. Being understanding also means being present for your spouse in their time of need - offering a listening ear and emotional support as they share their heart and their feelings. It's about being strong, spiritually aware, and available.

Alan's Perspective:

Being more understanding starts with being a good listener. Pay attention to what your spouse is saying without interrupting or assuming. Let them speak freely and avoid placing your own words or interpretations in their mouth.

Be sensitive to your spouse's tone and emotions. Show patience by allowing them the time to express their thoughts. Embrace the mindset that anything your spouse chooses to communicate is meaningful - even if it may not seem important to you at first.

You can't dictate how your spouse feels. Understanding begins with honoring their emotions, asking clarifying questions, and making necessary adjustments to foster peace. Your goal is to hear clearly, understand sincerely, and respond respectfully.

Our Perspective:

- Improving your listening skills will aid in being more understanding.
- Show how much you understand by taking your spouse's feelings seriously.
- Each spouse should make understanding the other a priority.
- Pray daily for wisdom regarding understanding in your marriage.
- Having and showing patience is a great way to become more understanding.

"Wisdom is the principal thing; therefore, get wisdom. And in all your getting, get understanding."
—*Proverbs 4:7 NKJV*

Reflection Questions:

1. When was the last time I truly listened to my spouse without interrupting or jumping to conclusions? What was the outcome?
2. Do I take time to understand my spouse's moods, communication style, and emotional needs? In what ways can I improve?
3. What does "being present" for my spouse look like in this season of our marriage?
4. Do I regularly ask God for wisdom and understanding in how to better support my spouse? If not, what's stopping me?
5. How do I respond when my spouse expresses something I disagree with or don't immediately understand? Is my response respectful and patient?

How Do You Instill Teamwork in Marriage?

Sobreta's Perspective:

Since marriage is the joining of two individuals becoming one, both spouses must be **committed to working together** toward a lasting and fulfilling partnership. Teamwork should be a top priority during both the planning and daily living stages of marriage.

Working as a team means **sharing responsibilities** in areas like finances, household chores, parenting, and even simple decisions like whether to cook at home or dine out. It also includes making **joint decisions** about critical matters such as health care, major purchases, where to live, and continuing education.

No one spouse should make major decisions independently unless it has already been agreed upon. For example, decisions like what to cook for dinner or spending from a designated allowance can be made individually if both spouses consent in advance. **The goal is agreement and alignment.** If there are disagreements, commit to finding a **sensible compromise** together. A marriage thrives when both partners actively contribute and respect one another's voice.

Alan's Perspective:

Teamwork in marriage is essential. It shows unity of purpose and a shared vision. To foster teamwork, you must first acknowledge that **both spouses have equal value and voice** in the relationship. No one partner should dominate or make unilateral decisions.

Avoid the mindset of "my way versus your way." Instead, ask: *What's best for us?* True teamwork emerges when both spouses feel heard, understood, and respected. When a couple consistently uses this approach - **open dialogue, mutual respect, and fair compromise** - the relationship becomes stronger and more unified.

The best decisions in marriage are the ones made together. That's how a team works: with honesty, humility, and shared responsibility.

Our Perspective:

- **Practice unity, togetherness, and trust** as core values in your marriage to build strong teamwork.
- **Both spouses have a voice,** and decisions should reflect mutual agreement and shared goals.
- **Work toward agreements** rather than pushing personal agendas.
- **Be intentional about compromise** and seek peaceful resolutions when disagreements arise.

"Two are better than one, because they have a good reward for their labor. For if they fall, one will lift up his companion. But woe to him who is alone when he falls, for he has no one to help him up." — Ecclesiastes 4:9–10 (NKJV)

Reflection Questions:

1. In what areas of our marriage do we already function well as a team? What makes those areas successful?
2. Are there responsibilities (e.g., finances, chores, parenting) that feel one-sided? How can we rebalance the load together?
3. How often do we make important decisions together? Are there times when one of us feels excluded?
4. What does "mutual agreement" look like in our marriage? Do we each feel heard and respected during decision-making?
5. How do we handle disagreements or opposing opinions? Do we seek compromise or push for our own way?
6. Do we celebrate our "wins" as a team—both big and small? How can we do a better job of acknowledging each other's contributions?

Does a Lack of Sexual Intimacy Mean Your Spouse Doesn't Love You?

Sobreta's Perspective:

Intimacy is more than physical - it's the feeling of closeness, connection, and emotional availability that deepens over time. A lack of physical intimacy doesn't necessarily mean your spouse doesn't love you. It may simply reflect how they are used to showing love. Not everyone is naturally affectionate or "touchy-feely," but that doesn't mean they are incapable of intimacy.

Intimacy can take many forms: shared laughter, intentional conversations, sitting close during a movie, or loving eye contact across the dinner table. Learn to observe and embrace the ways your spouse naturally expresses love. Over time, as trust builds and emotional bonds strengthen, expressions of intimacy - both emotional and physical - tend to grow.

If sexual intimacy is lacking, open up a conversation without accusation. Seek understanding before jumping to conclusions. And if needed, don't hesitate to get professional support to help restore what may have been lost. Remember, intimacy doesn't have to start with sex, but healthy intimacy can certainly lead to greater sexual connection.

Alan's Perspective:

A lack of sexual intimacy doesn't mean you don't love your spouse - but if left unaddressed, it can create serious strain in the marriage. Sex is designed to express and seal the oneness of marriage. Without it, you may still love your spouse, but you're missing a core part of what binds you emotionally and spiritually.

That said, frequency and expression may vary. If there's *some* sexual intimacy but frustration over how often it happens, that doesn't mean love is absent. It may be time to dig deeper: is the issue physical?

Medical? Mental? Emotional? Something as simple as attraction or personal hygiene can play a role, and these topics need to be addressed with honesty and grace.

Ask the uncomfortable questions. "What would you like to see me in?" "How would you like me to smell?" Don't just assume everything is okay, check in. Sexual intimacy is about meeting each other's needs, and that starts with communication.

Our Perspective:

- A lack of sexual intimacy doesn't automatically mean a lack of love—but it's still a serious issue that should be addressed.
- If it's due to a physical or medical challenge, seek professional help together.
- **Don't ignore** the emotional or mental components; patience and empathy go a long way.
- **Create space** for open, judgment-free conversations about expectations, desires, and what excites you both.
- **Learn to understand and appreciate** how your spouse naturally expresses love—even if it's different from your own style.
- **Remember**: intimacy begins with connection. Rebuild that, and physical intimacy can follow.

"Let the husband render to his wife the affection due her, and likewise also the wife to her husband." —1 Corinthians 7:3 (NKJV)

Reflection Questions:

1. In what ways does my spouse naturally express love, and have I taken time to appreciate those expressions?
2. Have I communicated my needs for physical intimacy in a loving and non-accusatory way?
3. Could outside factors (stress, health, emotions) be affecting our intimacy? Have we taken time to talk about them?

4. How do I define intimacy, and does my definition leave room for emotional and non-sexual forms of connection?
5. What small, intentional actions can I take to reignite closeness and trust with my spouse?
6. Have I made space for my spouse to express their needs and feelings without fear of criticism or pressure?
7. Would we benefit from seeking counsel or professional support to help restore intimacy in our relationship?

How Can We Improve Our Intimacy or Take It to the Next Level?

Sobreta's Perspective:

Improving intimacy begins with unity - being on one accord in heart, mind, and purpose. Intimacy can't thrive where selfishness or guilt-tripping exists. If your spouse isn't in the mood for physical intimacy, don't make them feel bad. Instead, focus on creating an atmosphere that welcomes closeness.

Intimacy is more than physical; it's about meeting emotional needs and showing genuine care. Sometimes, that looks like running a bubble bath, giving a foot or back rub, or offering your undivided attention during a quiet, cuddly moment. A heartfelt hug or soft kiss can deepen your connection without a single word.

Pay attention to your spouse's nonverbal cues and their efforts to connect, especially when they do something outside of their comfort zone just because they know it matters to you. That kind of intentionality builds intimacy naturally.

Also, avoid things that hinder intimacy: unresolved conflict, poor communication, or negative emotions. Be intentional and purposeful in creating a marriage where intimacy can flourish.

Alan's Perspective:

Taking intimacy to the next level starts with knowing what pleases your spouse. That means open communication about likes, dislikes, and boundaries. There's no growth in intimacy without mutual understanding and mutual respect.

Not everything your spouse enjoys will appeal to you - and that's okay. But it's important to find middle ground so that both of you experience pleasure and connection. Never force intimacy or introduce anything that violates your spouse's comfort or values. And never invite anyone else into your intimacy because this sacred connection is for you two alone.

Get creative but stay within the boundaries you've both agreed on. Weekly date nights are a powerful way to reconnect - whether it's a movie at home or a dinner out. Vacations or spontaneous weekend getaways help refresh your bond and reset your focus on one another.

Even simple things can deepen intimacy. For example, if your wife doesn't enjoy football but sits beside you watching a game and showing interest, that's powerful. Her effort speaks volumes—and you should do the same in return.

Our Perspective:

- **Prioritize your spouse and your marriage intentionally.** That's the foundation of stronger intimacy.
- **Schedule regular date nights**—be intentional and consistent.
- **Take budget-friendly trips** or spontaneous getaways to build lasting memories and deepen connection.
- **Learn each other's needs** and work to meet them—emotionally, physically, and spiritually.
- **Do things together** that one of you enjoys, even if the other isn't naturally interested. The effort speaks volumes.
- **New shared experiences** can ignite passion and deepen your intimacy. Be open to trying new things—together.

"I belong to my beloved, and his desire is for me."— Song of Solomon 7:10 (NIV)

Reflection Questions:

1. What specific actions make me feel most emotionally connected to my spouse? Have I shared that with them?
2. Are there any unspoken needs or desires I've been hesitant to express regarding our intimacy? How well do I respond to my spouse's nonverbal cues or emotional needs for closeness?

3. What distractions or barriers (e.g., unresolved conflict, busyness, resentment) are currently affecting our intimacy?
4. How can we make physical and emotional intimacy a regular part of our marriage, not just an occasional occurrence?

How Do We Overcome Infidelity in a Marriage?

Sobreta's Perspective:

Overcoming infidelity in marriage is not easy, but it is possible—**with genuine remorse, forgiveness, and commitment** to healing. The spouse who committed infidelity must be truly remorseful and **seek forgiveness with humility and sincerity**. This means more than just saying "I'm sorry." True repentance is demonstrated by a change in behavior, honest communication, and a desire to repair the damage done.

The wounded spouse must be willing to at least try to forgive, and this often requires **the help of the Holy Spirit**. Forgiveness does not mean forgetting, nor does it mean instant reconciliation. It is a spiritual process that begins with prayer and the decision to release bitterness.

Infidelity doesn't always mean the marriage is over, and it doesn't always mean the offending spouse wanted out. Sometimes, the enemy exploits a moment of weakness, temptation, or spiritual neglect. A lack of prayer, failure to set healthy boundaries, or neglecting time with your spouse can open doors to sin.

However, there **are couples who have overcome infidelity** and come out stronger on the other side. Healing is possible when there is **true repentance, intentional forgiveness, and both spouses working together** toward restoration.

Alan's Perspective:

Infidelity is **one of the hardest challenges** a marriage can face, but it's not impossible to overcome. The first and most critical step is that **both spouses must truly want to stay together and repair the marriage**. Without that shared desire, progress is nearly impossible.

Marriage is a **lifelong covenant**, and while infidelity breaks trust, it doesn't have to destroy the covenant - unless you allow it to. If the choice is to work through the betrayal, then **seek professional counseling immediately** - not from someone who will take sides, but from a neutral, experienced counselor. **Spiritual counseling is just as necessary** because this is also a spiritual battle.

Healing takes time. **There is no quick fix**, and the timeline cannot be rushed. Trust has been broken, and trust must be slowly and steadily rebuilt through transparency, patience, and love. Let your spouse go at their own pace. **You cannot force healing or forgiveness**.

Unfortunately, there are times when the pain is too deep, and one spouse may choose to walk away. If that happens, you must still seek personal healing. **You cannot control your spouse's decision**, but you are responsible for your own emotional and spiritual health moving forward.

Our Perspective:

- **Complete honesty** is the first step toward rebuilding trust.
- **Reestablish prayer and spiritual intimacy** in the marriage—pray together and for each other.
- **Be patient with the process**; trust-building takes time and effort from both sides.
- **Forgiveness is a process**—allow it to unfold without forcing or rushing.
- **Seek counseling together** with a professional therapist who supports both parties equally.

"Brothers, if anyone is caught in any transgression, you who are spiritual should restore him in a spirit of gentleness. Keep watch on yourself, lest you too be tempted." —Galatians 6:1 (ESV)

Reflection Questions:

1. Am I (or is my spouse) truly remorseful and willing to take consistent steps toward healing and restoration?

2. What boundaries or habits need to be put in place to prevent this from happening again?
3. Have we made space for honest, judgment-free conversations about what led to infidelity?
4. Am I willing to seek outside help, such as spiritual and professional counseling, to guide our healing process?
5. What does forgiveness look like for me right now? Am I willing to begin the process, even if it feels slow or difficult?
6. Are we both committed to rebuilding trust through transparency, prayer, and mutual effort?
7. How can I focus on my own healing while also supporting the healing of our marriage?

How Should a Married Couple Handle Household Responsibilities?

Sobreta's Perspective:

Handling household responsibilities is something both spouses should take seriously. As partners, you should each want to maintain a clean and orderly home and be willing to take responsibility for yourselves. While cleaning may not be a favorite activity for everyone, once two people come together in marriage, there should be a shift toward teamwork and shared effort.

One spouse may naturally be more skilled or inclined to clean than the other, but it's important to talk about expectations early on—ideally before marriage. Believe it or not, some marriages have faced serious challenges due to ongoing issues around cleanliness and imbalance in chores. To avoid this, consider making a weekly schedule that outlines household responsibilities for each person. Sharing the load helps prevent resentment and keeps things running smoothly.

In marriages where one spouse is the primary breadwinner and the other stays at home—often the husband works while the wife stays home—it's usually assumed that the stay-at-home spouse will manage most of the household tasks. Still, that person is not a servant. Respect and appreciation must always be shown. A kind gesture like picking up after yourself or asking how you can help goes a long way in showing love and partnership.

When there are children living in the home, they too should be given responsibilities that match their age and ability. Teaching them to keep their rooms tidy and help with tasks around the house instills values of responsibility and teamwork. I like to keep a simple chore calendar for our kids that rotates kitchen and bathroom duties - it's a great way to keep everyone involved and accountable.

Alan's Perspective:

Household responsibilities should be shared by everyone in the home - not just between husband and wife, but with the children too. Marriage is a team effort and so is running a household. When each person contributes, it builds unity and teaches valuable lessons, especially to the kids. It's not about who does more; it's about doing your part and supporting one another.

It's helpful to take stock of what each person naturally enjoys or does well. If someone loves to cook, let them take the lead in the kitchen. If another is great at organizing or cleaning, that can be their area of strength. When more than one person enjoys the same task, they can share the responsibility or take turns. **That's how teams work - by balancing one another out.**

Children should be encouraged to take care of their personal space, like keeping their rooms tidy, and pitch in with common areas too. Even outdoor tasks, like yard work or gardening, can become fun when done together as a family. If someone struggles with a certain chore, don't assign blame - just take time to teach them. **A little guidance can go a long way.**

The goal is to prevent burnout. No one person should carry the whole load, because eventually that can lead to frustration or feeling unappreciated. Be intentional about creating balance and hold each other accountable with love and respect. When everyone does their part, the home functions better, and the relationships within it grow stronger.

Our Perspective:

- Household responsibilities should be approached as a **shared effort** between spouses—and children if applicable.
- Communication and **clear expectations** can prevent future conflict.

- It's important to **acknowledge each other's strengths**, be flexible, and practice teamwork.
- Children should be included in maintaining the home to build **character and responsibility**.
- One person should never carry the full load—**balance prevents burnout** and cultivates appreciation.
- Doing chores together isn't just about cleanliness; it's about **serving each other in love**.

"Two are better than one, because they have a good return for their labor:" — *Ecclesiastes 4:9 (NIV)*

"Serve one another humbly in love." — *Galatians 5:13c (NIV)*

"Whatever you do, work at it with all your heart, as working for the Lord, not for human masters." — *Colossians 3:23 (NIV)*

Reflection Questions:

1. Have we clearly communicated our expectations around chores and household duties?
2. Do we both feel that the current division of responsibilities is fair and balanced? Why or why not?
3. Are there any tasks that consistently cause tension or resentment in our home? How can we address those as a team?
4. Do we regularly show appreciation for each other's efforts in maintaining the home?
5. Have we identified and assigned tasks based on each person's strengths and preferences? What practical steps can we take to improve our household routines, such as creating a schedule, rotating tasks, or working together more often?

How Should We Discipline Our Children When We Were Raised Differently?

Sobreta's Perspective:

I believe this is a great question for discussion. A married couple should share openly and honestly how they were raised and how they both would prefer to discipline their children. The most important thing is to agree on and teach the child(ren) the same morals and values that both spouses share. One spouse may not want to discipline the same way their parents disciplined them, and that is okay.

Since every child is different, the same methods of discipline may not work on each child. Some children do not need stern discipline in order to behave. Some children will behave without needing to be spanked, and some children will only behave after you've yelled at them a few times. Discussing how you're **not** going to discipline your children will also help. Setting boundaries around what is off-limits in your home (such as yelling, spanking, or isolation) can help both parents stay aligned.

Alan's Perspective:

This will definitely take patience, compromise, and communication - especially with blended families. When kids come into the picture, discipline is often shaped by the culture we were raised in. Some cultures took a physical approach to discipline, while others leaned toward non-physical correction.

This topic must be approached carefully, because if there's no unity between parents, it can cause serious division. In today's society, there are laws in place that prohibit many forms of physical discipline. In my opinion, non-physical methods should always be the first option. It helps keep the law out of your home, keeps your children safe, and still teaches discipline effectively.

That said, kids are smart. Some will test boundaries and even use legal protections to their advantage as they grow older. So, what about the parent who believes in a sterner approach? This is where communication and compromise are essential. You must talk and decide together if and when a firmer method is necessary - without immediately resorting to physical discipline.

I suggest starting by removing privileges. Many kids today are highly privileged from a young age, which is fine when they're respectful and responsible - but dangerous if they're disobedient. It's not wise to reward bad behavior. Set a standard in your home and teach your kids what's expected of them - respect, responsibility, and good behavior.

When they stray from these values, have a united conversation with them. If the behavior continues, escalate the discipline, but do it wisely. Reduce luxuries down to only what's needed, not what's wanted. That can be more effective than physical punishment.

And if none of these works, then seek professional help. Your family is too important to risk division because of different parenting styles. Be patient and work together until you learn to parent your children as one.

Our Perspective:

- **Talk** early and often about how you were raised and how that shapes your view of discipline.
- **Agree** on your core values and what you want to instill in your children.
- **Present a united front**—never argue about discipline in front of your kids.
- **Decide together** what forms of discipline are acceptable and what's off-limits.
- **Discipline** with the goal of teaching, not punishing.
- **Be consistent, loving, and intentional.**

"Discipline your children, and they will give you peace; they will bring you the delights you desire."
— *Proverbs 29:17 (NIV)*

Reflection Questions:

1. What discipline methods were used in your childhood? How did they affect you?
2. Which parts of your upbringing would you like to carry into your parenting? Which would you rather leave behind?
3. Have we discussed and agreed on what forms of discipline we will (and will not) use?
4. How do we respond when we disagree on how to handle a behavior issue?
5. Are we consistently reinforcing the same values and consequences as a united front?
6. What is one step we can take to improve our communication and unity around discipline?

How Important Is Financial Stability in Marriage?

Sobreta's Perspective:

Maintaining financial stability is crucial for every individual, and even more so within the context of marriage. If not handled properly, finances can quickly become a source of instability and tension in the relationship. How a couple will manage their finances should be discussed and agreed upon before marriage.

Getting financial counseling together is a great way to ensure you're on the same page when it comes to budgeting, spending habits, saving, and paying bills. Everyone's financial background and upbringing are different, so it's essential to understand each other's experiences with money.

It's also important that each person has demonstrated the ability to live independently and responsibly before entering marriage. Knowing how to manage basic responsibilities like rent, electricity, and water bills on time is essential.

Decide together who will be responsible for which bills and how much each will contribute. Write out a financial plan and stick to it—but remain flexible enough to revise it as needed. Resolving financial issues together can actually draw you closer as a couple when love and respect are present.

Alan's Perspective:

Establishing financial stability in marriage is very important. It begins with honest communication and setting realistic financial goals together. From there, create a plan that reflects those goals and begin working toward them as a team.

There is no one-size-fits-all method when it comes to managing money in marriage. Whether you choose joint accounts, separate accounts, or a combination—do what works best for your marriage. If one of you is stronger at managing finances, it may make sense for that person to take the lead. If you're both capable, work together. If one spouse prefers not to handle finances at all, and both agree to that arrangement, that can work too.

What matters most is agreement. When both spouses are in unity regarding how finances are handled, it builds trust and helps avoid unnecessary conflict.

Our Perspective:

- **Come to an agreement** on how to handle finances.
- **Always communicate** money situations, financial concerns, and future goals.
- **Don't live beyond your financial means or obligations.**
- **Do not allow financial issues to destroy your marriage.**

"Wisdom is a shelter as money is a shelter, but the advantage of knowledge is this: Wisdom preserves those who have it." - Ecclesiastes 7:12 (NIV)

Reflection Questions:

1. Are we in agreement about how to manage our finances (e.g., budgeting, saving, giving, spending)?
2. Have we discussed whether to use joint or separate accounts—and do we both feel heard in that decision?
3. Do we have a plan in place for handling financial emergencies or unexpected expenses?
4. How do we currently communicate about money—and how can we improve that communication?
5. Are there any unspoken financial tensions or past mistakes that we need to address openly?

How Important Are Parents to Your Relationship?

Sobreta's Perspective:

Parents are crucial because, quite simply, they are the reason you're here. While the Bible teaches that a man should *leave his father and mother and cleave to his wife* (Genesis 2:24), we must also acknowledge the foundational role parents play in shaping us. They help prepare us emotionally, spiritually, and even practically for marriage.

As couples grow together, they often carry lessons - both good and bad - from their upbringing into their own relationship. For some, their parents modeled a strong, loving marriage. For others, the goal might be to create a healthier environment than the one they experienced growing up. Either way, **valuable lessons can be learned**.

It's a blessing when parents are still around to offer guidance or support, especially as you raise your own children. But their involvement should never take precedence over your marriage. It's okay to seek their wisdom, but **your spouse comes first**. Set healthy boundaries early on to protect your relationship. Your marriage should never be built around your parents' preferences or expectations, but rather around God's plan for the two of you.

Alan's Perspective:

Parents play an important role in your life - but once you're married, that role shifts. Before marriage, parents are the central figures of influence. But marriage restructures your priorities. **Now, your spouse becomes your first priority**.

Mark 10:6-9 (NKJV) reminds us that when two become one flesh, no one, including parents, should come between that union. We're still called to **honor our parents**, but not at the expense of our spouse or family unit.

It's perfectly fine to receive wisdom and support from parents. But the final decision in your home belongs to you and your spouse. Parents should **never be allowed to control or interfere with your marriage**. And they definitely should not be used as leverage between spouses.

Remember, just because something worked for your parents doesn't mean it will work for you. Your marriage is **a unique creation**. Let God shape it specifically for you and your household.

Our Perspective:

- Parents are **important and deserve honor**, but your spouse comes **first after God**.
- Healthy boundaries with parents protect the **unity and intimacy of your marriage**.
- Seek advice from your parents if you trust their wisdom but **make final decisions as a couple**.
- Never allow a parent's opinion to override your spouse's voice in your marriage.
- Understand that **every marriage is different** - what worked for your parents might not work for you.
- **Do not allow negativity, manipulation, or control** from parents to interfere with your relationship.
- Aim to **learn from the past**, whether good or bad, to build a marriage that honors God and each other.

"Honor your father and your mother, that your days may be long in the land that the LORD your God is giving you." —Exodus 20:12 (ESV)

Reflection Questions:

1. How have our relationships with our parents shaped the way we approach marriage?
2. Do either of us struggle with setting healthy boundaries with our parents? If so, how can we address that together?

3. Have we ever allowed a parent's opinion to override what's best for our relationship? How did that affect us?
4. Are we in agreement about how much involvement our parents should have in our marriage or family decisions?
5. How can we honor our parents while still protecting the unity and privacy of our marriage?
6. Are there any past experiences with our parents (positive or negative) that we still need to process together?
7. How can we ensure that our marriage is being shaped more by God's direction than by parental expectations?

Should a Married Couple Be Members of the Same Church?

Sobreta's Perspective:

In my opinion, it is a beautiful thing when families worship together in the same church. It's important for a married couple to be under the same spiritual covering, receiving the same teachings and messages week after week. If a couple wasn't already attending the same church when they met, this should be a conversation once they're married. They should seek God together in prayer, asking for guidance about where He would have them worship and grow together.

Since marriage is a union where two become one, that unity should also be reflected in their spiritual life. Being planted in one church home is a visible sign of togetherness and shared faith. Of course, there are couples who worship in different churches and still manage to maintain healthy marriages. This usually works best when they share the same core beliefs and have their relationship grounded in Christ.

But there's something truly powerful about being in the same room, lifting up praises together, hearing the same word, and being strengthened as a spiritual team. At the end of the day, a family that prays together really does stay together.

Alan's Perspective:

In my opinion, a couple can survive spiritually while attending different churches - if the core beliefs, doctrine, and foundation of their faith are aligned. I know couples who've done just that and are still thriving in their marriages. That said, I believe it's far better and more effective to worship under the same roof.

Being part of the same church creates spiritual cohesiveness. It deepens your sense of unity as a couple and as a family. You grow together through the same word, you're held accountable by the same leadership, and you serve in the same environment. That kind of togetherness strengthens both your faith and your bond.

It doesn't have to be a major issue if you're starting from different churches, as long as there's honest communication and a willingness to compromise. Still, from my experience and perspective, unity in worship adds another layer of strength to the marriage - it's just better to be united on all fronts.

Our Perspective:

- **Worshiping together** as a couple can strengthen spiritual unity and deepen the marriage bond.
- Being under the same church leadership and teaching helps ensure both spouses grow together spiritually.
- Attending separate churches may work for some couples, but it's not ideal for long-term unity.
- **Couples should pray and seek God's guidance** about where to worship together as one.
- **Sharing the same foundational beliefs** is essential, regardless of church membership.
- **Communication and compromise** are key if starting from different church homes.
- A family that prays, worships, and grows together is more likely to stay strong and unified.

"Again I say to you that if two of you agree on earth concerning anything that they ask, it will be done for them by My Father in heaven. For where two or three are gathered together in My name, I am there in the midst of them." —Matthew 18:19–20 (NKJV) - Highlights the power and presence of God when couples pray and worship together in unity.

"Endeavoring to keep the unity of the Spirit in the bond of peace." — Ephesians 4:3 (NKJV) - Speaks to the spiritual bond and peace that comes from unity, including within marriage.

"Not forsaking the assembling of ourselves together, as is the manner of some, but exhorting one another - and so much the more as you see the Day approaching." —Hebrews 10:25 (NKJV) - Encourages regular, shared fellowship in the body of Christ.

Reflection Questions:

1. Are we currently worshiping in the same church? If not, how is that affecting our spiritual connection?
2. Have we taken time to pray and seek God's direction about where we should worship as a couple?
3. Do we share the same foundational beliefs, even if our church backgrounds differ?
4. How important is it to us to grow spiritually together in a shared church environment?
5. What are some ways we can strengthen our spiritual unity if attending different churches?
6. Are we both open and willing to compromise in choosing a church that supports our marriage and faith?

Can People with Different Religious Beliefs Have a Successful Marriage?

Sobreta's Perspective:

The Bible says, "Be ye not unequally yoked," and "How can two walk together except they agree?" Walking together reflects unity, agreement, and shared direction. When two people don't agree on something as central as their faith, it can create confusion and make it difficult to move forward in harmony. God desires unity and peace in our relationships, especially in marriage.

For a marriage to thrive, it helps greatly when both partners share the same faith and values. When there are significant differences—such as differing beliefs about who Jesus is or whether God established marriage—it can be hard to find common ground in key areas like worship, parenting, or decision-making.

While it may be possible for people with different beliefs to love each other and make their relationship work in some ways, having a shared spiritual foundation offers a deeper sense of connection and purpose. It brings clarity, direction, and strength to the relationship.

From our perspective, a strong and lasting marriage is built on a solid foundation—and for us, that foundation is faith in Jesus Christ. We believe that when both husband and wife are united in their belief in Him, they are better equipped to navigate life's challenges together and build a marriage that honors God and stands the test of time.

Alan's Perspective:

It really depends on how you define a successful marriage. While it's true that two people of different religious backgrounds may find ways to live peacefully and respectfully with one another, a truly God-honoring marriage—one that is spiritually united and blessed by God—requires more than coexistence.

In 2 Corinthians 6:14 (NKJV), the Bible advises us not to be unequally yoked with unbelievers. This verse speaks to the importance of spiritual unity in close relationships, especially marriage. Similarly, Mark 10:7-8 describes marriage as two becoming one flesh. That kind of oneness goes beyond emotional and physical connection—it involves spiritual alignment as well.

God created marriage, and He designed it to function in a particular way. For a marriage to thrive under His blessing, it must align with His Word. That means both spouses need to walk together in faith, submitting to God and supporting one another in spiritual growth.

When one person believes in Jesus Christ and the other does not, it can create division in values, priorities, and decision-making. Those differences can challenge the unity God desires for marriage. It's not about judgment—it's about wisdom and alignment. God knows what's best for us, and He calls us to be equally yoked so that we can walk in unity and receive the full blessings of His design for marriage.

Our Perspective:

- A truly successful marriage - **one that honors God and endures**—requires spiritual unity.
- **Being equally yoked** means sharing the same faith, values, and foundational beliefs, especially regarding Jesus Christ and God's design for marriage.
- Having different religious beliefs can lead to **division in major areas** of life, such as parenting, worship, decision-making, and moral values.
- God is the author of marriage; therefore, **a marriage that excludes Him or misaligns with His Word may struggle to receive His blessings**.
- Coexisting with different beliefs may offer **temporary peace**, but it doesn't equate to the **oneness** God desires in marriage.
- **Unity in faith builds a stronger foundation** for enduring trials, raising children, and growing together spiritually and emotionally.

- For the best chance at a blessed and lasting marriage, couples should pursue **spiritual alignment from the beginning**.

14 Do not be unequally yoked together with unbelievers. For what fellowship has righteousness with lawlessness? And what communion has light with darkness? 15 And what accord has Christ with Belial? Or what part has a believer with an unbeliever? 16 And what agreement has the temple of God with idols? For you[f] are the temple of the living God. As God has said: "I will dwell in them and walk among them. I will be their God, and they shall be My people." —2 Corinthians 6:14,15 (NKJV)

6 But from the beginning of the creation, God 'made them male and female.' 7 'For this reason a man shall leave his father and mother and be joined to his wife, 8 and the two shall become one flesh'; so then they are no longer two, but one flesh. 9 Therefore what God has joined together, let not man separate." —Mark 10:6-9 (NKJV)

Reflection Questions:

1. Are we truly aligned in our core beliefs about God, Jesus, and the purpose of marriage?
2. How do our individual faiths influence our decisions, parenting, and daily life together?
3. In what ways has our shared (or differing) faith helped - or challenge our sense of unity as a couple?
4. Are we intentionally growing together spiritually, or are we walking separate paths in our faith?
5. How can we better pursue spiritual alignment to build a stronger, God-honoring marriage?

Closing Prayer

Heavenly Father,

We thank You for the sacred gift of marriage and the divine covenant it represents. As we close this book, we open our hearts to You - inviting Your presence, wisdom, and grace into every corner of our relationship. Strengthen our commitment to one another and to You. Help us to love with patience, serve with humility, and forgive with mercy.

Lord, where there is brokenness, bring healing. Where there is distance, draw us closer. Where there is uncertainty, give us clarity and peace. Let our marriage reflect Your love, a love that is enduring, sacrificial, and eternal.

We declare that our union is not just personal, but purposeful. Let our lives together be a testimony of Your faithfulness and power. Teach us to walk in unity, honor, and spiritual alignment, fully surrendered to Your will.

Bless every married couple who reads this book. May they find strength in their struggles, joy in their journey, and confidence in Your promises. Help them to build marriages that are rooted in Christ and committed for a lifetime.

Bless engaged couples as they prepare to join their lives in marriage. Fill their hearts with love, understanding, and unity. Guide them to build a strong foundation grounded in You, so they may face life's joys and challenges together with grace and faith. May their union reflect Your love and bring You glory.

And finally, we lift up every heart longing for a spouse. Strengthen their faith and patience as they wait on Your perfect timing. Prepare their heart and the heart of their future partner and guide them to a love rooted in You. Help them to trust Your plan and to grow in joy and purpose while they wait.

In Jesus' name we pray,
Amen.

Prayers for Your Marriage

No matter where you are in your marriage, prayer is your greatest weapon and most powerful tool. These prayers are designed to guide your heart, refocus your perspective, and invite God's healing presence into your relationship. Take your time. Sit with them. Let the Lord speak—and then write your own below each one.

A Prayer for Unity

Lord, bring our hearts together as one. Teach us to communicate with love, forgive with grace, and walk in step with Your Spirit. Let our unity reflect Your covenant. In Jesus' Name, amen.

Your Prayer or Reflection:

_____

_____

_____

_____

_____

_____

A Prayer for Emotional Healing

Father, heal every wound we've caused each other - spoken and unspoken. Restore our joy, rebuild our trust, and renew the intimacy that once was. Let Your love be the glue that holds us together. In Jesus' Name, amen.

Your Prayer or Reflection:

_____

_____

_____

_____

_____

A Prayer for Intimacy

God, help us to connect deeply - spiritually, emotionally, and physically. Remove walls of discomfort, fear, or offense. Let passion and peace flourish in our bedroom and beyond. In Jesus' Name, amen.

Your Prayer or Reflection:

_____

_____

_____

_____

A Prayer for Wisdom

Lord, give us the wisdom to lead, love, and live well together. Help us make decisions that honor You and strengthen our bond. Let Your truth guide our every step. In Jesus' Name, amen.

Your Prayer or Reflection:

A Prayer for Stubborn Love

Jesus, when it's hard to love, help us choose love anyway. When it's easier to shut down or walk away, remind us of our vows. When it's easier to use harsh and hurtful words, helps us to honor our spouse with respect. Let our love reflect Yours - unconditional, patient, and enduring. In Jesus' Name, amen.

Your Prayer or Reflection:

A Prayer for Forgiveness

Jesus, when it's hard to forgive, help us to remember that You are a forgiving Father, and it is Your will that we walk in forgiveness. When it's easier to hold a grudge, help us to remember that we are imperfect people and we are prone to make mistakes. Help us to not hold our unintentional actions against each other. Let Your Holy Spirit guide us to lovingly forgive as we strive to understand each other's differences. In Jesus' Name, amen.

A Prayer for a Blended Family

Father, thank You for our unique family. Give us grace to navigate the layers of love, history, and expectations. Help us lead with unity, patience, and wisdom. Let peace fill our home and love cover every difference. Amen.

Your Prayer or Reflection:

A Prayer for a Spouse Who Is Unsaved

Lord, I lift up my spouse to You. Open their heart to Your truth and draw them close. Use my life as a light that points to You. Give me strength to love without condition and to trust You with the journey. In Jesus' name, amen.

Your Prayer or Reflection:

_____

_____

_____

_____

_____

_____

_____

✍ Notes & Reflections

Use the pages below for your own prayers, journal entries, or anything God speaks to you during this journey.

Page 1:

Page 2:

Page 3:

Conclusion

Marriage is a sacred journey - one filled with seasons of joy, growth, testing, and triumph. As you've read through these pages, our hope is that you've been reminded that you are not alone. God is with you, and He desires for your marriage to thrive - not just survive.

Whether you are newly married, rebuilding after hardship, or simply seeking to grow closer as a couple, know that every step taken in faith brings you closer to the covenant God designed for you. Stay rooted in His Word, committed to each other, and open to continual growth.

We believe that when two hearts are fully surrendered to God and each other, no challenge is too great, and no dream is out of reach.

Remain forever committed - to God, to one another, and to the purpose He has for your union.

With love and grace,
Alan & Sobreta Harris
Forever Committed Marriage Ministry

About the Authors

Alan and Sobreta Harris are licensed ministers who have been joyfully married since February 2002. Their journey began in New Orleans, Louisiana, where they met while attending Greater St. Stephen Full Gospel Baptist Church under the leadership of Bishop Paul S. Morton, Sr. From the start, it was clear their connection was more than personal - it was rooted in a shared calling to serve and strengthen marriages through faith.

As a blended family with six now-grown children, Alan and Sobreta have experienced both the joys and challenges of marriage, parenting, and ministry. Even before they met, Sobreta received a prophetic word that she would one day minister to couples alongside her husband. At the time, Alan was already ministering to men, and Sobreta was actively serving in various areas, including women's ministry, helps ministry and evangelism. As their relationship deepened, their shared calling became undeniable. Whether in everyday conversations or more intentional settings, couples often turned to them for encouragement and guidance. These encounters confirmed their God-given purpose: to support and strengthen marriages with honesty, compassion, and biblical truth.

Following Hurricane Katrina, the Harrises relocated to Houston, Texas, where they joined Greater Antioch Full Gospel Baptist Church under Bishop Lester Love and later joined Harvest Time Church under Bishop Shelton Bady, where they served on the evangelism team, sang in the choir and on the praise team. From 2008 to 2016, they faithfully served in the Marriage Ministry - facilitating classes, mentoring couples (premarital and marital), and investing deeply in the spiritual and emotional health of marriages. It was during this time that the vision for Forever Committed Marriage Ministry began to take shape.

Their own marriage stands as a testimony to God's faithfulness and the power of covenant. From the beginning, they made a firm decision that divorce would never be an option. That foundation has carried them through life's challenges and strengthened their resolve to help others build lasting, God-honoring unions.

Forever Committed is both a ministry and a mission, born from years of experience, spiritual insight, and a passion to see marriages thrive. This book is an outgrowth of that mission, and it is their heartfelt prayer that it brings encouragement, strength, and renewed purpose to your own marital journey.

Alan & Sobreta Harris are licensed ministers, marriage mentors, and the founders of *Forever Committed Marriage Ministry*. Their passion is to help couples build strong, Christ-centered marriages rooted in truth, faith, and covenant love.

"We believe in love that lasts, truth that heals, and commitment that reflects Christ."

✉ forevercommittedmm@gmail.com

Facebook: 👤 facebook.com/alanandsobreta

www.ingramcontent.com/pod-product-compliance
Lightning Source LLC
Chambersburg PA
CBHW070601170426
43201CB00012B/1891